PAMPHLETS ON AMERICAN WRITERS · NUMBER 27

UNIVERSITY OF MINNESOTA

D1312146

⌁ *Sinclair Lewis*

BY MARK SCHORER

UNIVERSITY OF MINNESOTA PRESS · MINNEAPOLIS

Printed in the United States of America at
the North Central Publishing Company, St. Paul

Library of Congress Catalog Card Number: 63-62713

The general evaluation of this essay is inevitably the
same as that of my book, *Sinclair Lewis: An American
Life,* and sometimes the language as well. When I re-
peat myself, I do so with the permission of the publishers, McGraw-Hill Book Co., Inc.   M. S.

Distributed to high schools in the United States by
McGraw-Hill Book Company, Inc.
New York   Chicago   Corte Madera, Calif.   Dallas

PUBLISHED IN GREAT BRITAIN, INDIA, AND PAKISTAN BY THE OXFORD
UNIVERSITY PRESS, LONDON, BOMBAY, AND KARACHI, AND IN
CANADA BY THOMAS ALLEN, LTD., TORONTO

SINCLAIR LEWIS

MARK SCHORER, professor of English in the University of California, Berkeley, is the author of three novels, many short stories, some works of literary criticism, and a biography of Sinclair Lewis.

↙ *Sinclair Lewis*

Harry Sinclair Lewis was the youngest of the three sons of a country doctor, Edwin J. Lewis. He was born on February 7, 1885, in the Minnesota village of Sauk Centre, a raw little town less than thirty years old. No one now knows where the name Harry came from, but the name Sinclair, which was to become famous, was the surname of a Wisconsin dentist who was Dr. Lewis' good friend. The boy's mother was an ailing woman who had to spend much of her time away from home, in the South and Southwest, and when Harry was five, she died. In a year the doctor was married again — to a good, brisk, busy woman well suited to the hard-working doctor's unbending, frugal temperament. Harry Lewis' boyhood was curiously loveless, vexatious.

He was homely, ill-coordinated, astigmatic, redheaded, a stumbling, noisy, awkward boy. He was inept at hunting and fishing, could hardly swim, was shunned in boys' games and sports, derided by his fellows and patronized by his elders. He was nearly friendless and was early given to solitary tramps about the countryside and to wide, indiscriminate reading. He yearned to be in some place both more colorful and more kindly than Sauk Centre.

When he was seventeen, his father, whose forebears had lived near New Haven, Connecticut, allowed him to enroll in Yale College after six months of necessary preparation in the Oberlin Academy. The college experience dashed his hopes for a happier life: at Yale he was again friendless and lonely, more the outsider than ever, even though a number of his professors, recognizing his lively intelligence, were good to him. In high school he had written occasional verses, and now at Yale he began to write regularly.

5

Writing was not only a substitute for those social amenities that were denied him but also, he saw, the one means available to him whereby he might win the recognition and the respect of his fellows.

His early verse and prose alike bore almost no resemblance at all to either the subjects or the manner for which he would ultimately become famous. The poetry was imitative, occasionally of Kipling but generally of Tennyson and Swinburne, and he was much given to medieval subjects as he conceived them. His prose was archaic and floriated and its subject matter fantastic and melodramatic. Still, in 1904, he was the only freshman at Yale to appear (with a poem called "Launcelot") in the *Yale Literary Magazine*. That poem is not without a certain imitative charm and almost certainly represents the highest poetic achievement of H. Sinclayre Lewys (as, at sixteen, he had thought of his literary persona).

wrote early

LAUNCELOT

"Oft Launcelot grieves that he loveth the Queen
But oftener far that she cruel hath been."

> Blow, weary wind,
> The golden rod scarce chiding;
> Sir Launcelot is riding
> By shady wood-paths pleasant
> To fields of yellow corn.
> He starts a whirring pheasant,
> And clearly winds his horn.
> The Queen's Tower gleams mid distant hills;
> A thought like joyous sunshine thrills,
> "My love grows kind."
>
> Blow, weary wind,
> O'er lakes, o'er dead swamps crying,
> Amid the gray stumps sighing
> While slow, and cold, and sullen,
> The waves splash on the shore.
> O'er wastes of bush and mullen,

6

Dull crows flap, evermore.
The Autumn day is chill and drear
As yon knight, thinking Guenevere
Proves most unkind.

Once this poem was accepted, the way was open for him on the *Lit.*
In the following years he became a regular contributor to this and
other undergraduate periodicals and in his third year the number
of his contributions won him a place on the editorial staff of the
Lit.

During two of his summers he made cattleboat trips to England
and on these trips he began to take systematic notes for fiction.
One summer he returned to Sauk Centre where excruciating bore-
dom led him to conceive of a novel to be called *The Village Virus.*
(When this novel was at last written, it was called *Main Street.*)
In spite of his literary success at college, life at Yale grew increasingly exasperating for him, and at the beginning of his senior year
he abruptly fled from New Haven to become a janitor and general
handyman at Helicon Hall, the odd experiment in communal
living that Upton Sinclair had just established near Englewood,
New Jersey, on the Palisades. He sustained that effort for about
a month.

Since in this recusant period his father was not giving him any
money at all, the young man went to New York determined to live
by his pen, but after several months of near starvation he left for
Panama where he hoped to find work on the canal then under
construction. That failing too he suddenly decided to return to
New Haven and finish his education at Yale. He was readmitted
to the College and he was graduated in June of 1908, a year behind
his class.

There followed a number of years of miscellaneous adventure
all over the United States, a time in which he tried to be a news-
paperman without success, and continued to try to publish without

7

much success. Iowa, New York, San Francisco, Washington, New York again. For a brief period he lived in a newly established bohemian colony in Carmel, California, where his associates were such writers as George Sterling and Jack London. Failing to sell his own stories, Lewis sold a number of plots (from the enormous plot file that he had put together) to London for sums ranging from five to fifteen dollars, but even this munificence on the part of the older writer could hardly be expected to support the younger and more inventive writer. From the end of 1910 until the end of 1915, he worked in publishing houses in New York and on a number of periodicals. During his vacation in one summer he wrote a boys' book, *Hike and the Aeroplane*, on commission for Frederick A. Stokes Company and published it under the pseudonym of Tom Graham.

More important, Lewis was all the time working on what would be his first novel, and although his friends in publishing circles discouraged him in his effort to be a serious novelist, he continued to work at it until he had what he thought was a publishable manuscript. After it was rejected by several publishers, it was accepted at last by the firm of Harpers and published in February of 1914. Two months later, on April 15, Lewis was married to his first wife, a young woman named Grace Livingstone Hegger who now gave up her employment in the office of *Vogue* to establish the first Lewis ménage in the Long Island community of Port Washington. Lewis was still working in Manhattan, writing furiously at home before and after work and on commuting trains, but he was always pining for the time when he could afford to live by writing alone.

Our Mr. Wrenn had a reasonably good press but very small sales. The second novel, *The Trail of the Hawk*, published in 1915, enjoyed the same fate. At work on a third novel, Lewis found suddenly that his whole situation was altered when the *Saturday*

Evening Post accepted his story called "Nature, Inc." This acceptance was quickly followed by three more, and Lewis was being paid $1000 for each story. With money in the bank for the first time in his life, he resigned his position at the Doran publishing house and in December of 1915 set out with his wife on what would be a life of wandering throughout their marriage. Traveling once more all over the United States, briefly setting up one residence and then another, he was writing literally scores of stories, almost all of them to be published in the slick periodicals, and he was also working at a number of books. The first of these, called *The Innocents*, was in fact planned as a magazine serial, and is one of the worst books he ever wrote. The next, though the first to be published as a book — both it and *The Innocents* appeared in 1917 — was titled *The Job*; it is one of the best of his early books. The fifth of his novels, called *Free Air*, is a sentimental fictionalization of the Lewis trip across the continent in a Ford, and was published in 1919. At the same time that he was finishing *Free Air*, Lewis was working at what would be *Main Street*, finished in Washington early in the summer of 1920 and published in the fall of that year. Now the apprenticeship was abruptly ended, and ended in a positive storm of vilification and applause. Suddenly Sinclair Lewis was a famous man.

When *Main Street* appeared, plunging literary America into a rare and heated controversy, it seemed that nothing like it, with its shrill indictment of village life, the middle class, provincial America, had been published before. For many years popular American fiction had been picturing village life as sweet and good, the middle class as kindly when not noble, the provinces as aglow with an innocence in sharp contrast to the cruelty and corruption of the cities. In the fifty years before 1920 there had, to be sure, been exceptions — novels a good deal more critical of village life than was the rule; but the prevailing view was that of Friendship

9

Village, and it was this view that *Main Street* abruptly and perhaps forever ended.

Main Street seemed to those readers who had known Lewis'
earlier work to be a complete rupture with everything he had done
before. A look at those earlier novels now shows this not to have
been the situation at all. All five works had essentially the same
pattern: the impulse to escape the conventions of class or routine;
flight; a partial success and a necessary compromise with convention. Realistic in detail, these novels were optimistic in tone in a
way that was not generally associated with what was then thought
of as the school of realism, and it was the combination of the optimistic view of human character with the body of observed social
detail that critics remarked and some readers enjoyed.

There had been satirical flashes in the earlier books if not the
generally sustained and less good-tempered satire of *Main Street*,
but satire nevertheless and satire directed against the same general
objects. Furthermore, when those earlier novels were effective,
they were so because of the body of closely observed physical detail,
but it was detail more impressionistically, less massively presented
than in *Main Street*. Certain character types that were to be made
famous by *Main Street* had already appeared — the hypocritical
bigot, the village atheist, the aspiring idealist, and so on. And the
basic pattern of *Main Street* was exactly the same pattern that has
already been described: a young creature is caught in a stultifying
environment, clashes with that environment, flees from it, is forced
to return, compromises.

Carol Kennicott, the heroine of *Main Street*, has no alternative
to compromise. Her values, her yearning for a free and gracious
life, had only the vaguest shape, and when she tried to put them
into action in Gopher Prairie, Minnesota, she found only the most
artificial and sentimental means. To some readers even then (when
thousands of women were identifying themselves with her) she

seemed like a rather foolish young woman, and so today she must seem to every reader. In the end, the true values are those of her husband, "Doc" Kennicott, who, for all his stolidity, is honest, hard-working, kindly, thrifty, motivated by common sense — altogether like Lewis' brother, Dr. Claude, and even rather like his father, Dr. E. J. It is Kennicott who has the last word. In the end, then, it is the middle class that triumphs and the Middle West, and the middle-brow. And so it would always be in fact in the novels of Sinclair Lewis.

It is more accurate to say that the triumph is given to the *best* qualities of the middle class and that it is its worst qualities that the novel castigates: smugness, hypocrisy, a gross materialism, moral cant. These are the qualities that Lewis' satire, even when the focus begins to blur as it does with *Dodsworth*, would continue to assail. Thus, immediately after *Main Street*, he plunged into his research in that section of American life where those qualities were most obvious and therefore most readily lampooned — the commercial world of the middle-class businessman in a medium-sized city. "Research" is the correct word if one thinks of a novelist operating in the fashion of a sociologist preparing to make a field report. It is the novel *Babbitt* that established what would henceforth be Sinclair Lewis' characteristic method of work, a method toward which he had been moving ever since his cattleboat note-taking days.

To begin, he chose a subject — not, as for most novelists, a character situation or a mere theme, but a social area that could be systematically studied and mastered. Ordinarily, this was a subclass within the middle class, a profession, or a particular problem of such a subclass. Then, armed with his notebooks, he mingled with the kind of people that his fiction would mainly concern. In Pullman cars and smokers, in the lobbies of side-street hotels, in athletic clubs, in a thousand junky streets he watched and listened,

11

and then meticulously copied into his notebooks whole catalogues of expressions drawn from the American lingo, elaborate lists of proper names, every kind of physical detail. He drew intricately detailed maps, and maps not only of the city in which his story was set but of the houses in which his actions would take place, floor plans with furniture precisely located, streets and the kind and color of dogs that walked on them. Mastering this body of material, he would then write out a summary of his story, and from this, a much more extended "plan," as he called it, with every scene sketched in, the whole sometimes nearly as long as the book that would come from it. A first draft would then follow, usually much longer than the final version, and then a long process of revision and cutting, and at last the publishable text. Although he traveled the length and breadth of the United States in 1920 and 1921, always listening and looking with *Babbitt* in mind, it was, in fact, Cincinnati, Ohio, that provided the chief scene of his researches for this novel about a place called Zenith.

Again, *Babbitt* (1922) plunged the nation into literary controversy. Again, the novel seemed absolutely new, unlike anything that had come before it. Again, to many the assault on American virtue seemed brutal, uncompromising, and unfair. All over the United States Sinclair Lewis was denounced as a villain and a traitor, and all over the United States thousands and thousands of people bought his novel. In Europe it seemed that someone in America was finally telling the whole truth about the appalling culture of that deplorable country. A class had been defined, as it had been given the name that stays with it still. H. L. Mencken's abstraction of *boobus Americanus* had been given a body, a body that lives still in the American imagination.

Lewis' original intention in *Babbitt*, he later said, was to recount twenty-four hours in the life of his character, "from alarm clock to alarm clock." That original structural conception remains in the first seven chapters as the book stands. The remaining twenty-seven chapters are systematically planned if rather aimlessly assembled set pieces that, taken together, give us the sociology of middle-class American life. These pieces have as their topics such matters as Politics, Leisure, Club Life, Trade Association Conventions, Class Structure and Attitudes, Conventional Religion, "Crank" Religion, Labor Relations, Marriage and the Family, and such lesser topics as The Barbershop and The Speakeasy. There is no plot to contain and unite these interests, but their fragmentariness is in part overcome by the fact that George Babbitt moves through all of them in the course of his rising discontent, his rebellion, his retreat and resignation. Each of these three moods, in turn, centers in a more or less separate narrative: the first in the imprisonment of Paul Riesling after he shoots his wife; the second in Babbitt's attempt to find sympathy in Tanis Judique and "the Bunch"; the third in the pressures brought on him by the Good Citizens' League and his wife's happily coincidental emergency operation. It is not surprising that the general thematic and narrative movement, like the central figure himself, is sometimes lost to sight in the forest of marshaled mores.

Had the early optimist vanished in the Menckenian pessimist, as it seemed to so many readers in 1922 and 1923? In fact, the essential narrative pattern had not changed in *Babbitt*: the individual trapped in an environment, catching glimmerings of something more desirable beyond it, struggling to grasp them, succeeding or failing. Babbitt fails — or nearly does — with the result that the comic-satiric element here is both heightened and broadened over that of the earlier novels. Clifton Fadiman, writing later, defined the essential pattern when he wrote of Dodsworth as a man who "can neither give himself wholly over to the business of *being* a businessman nor give himself wholly over to the more difficult business of being a man. His vacillation between the part and the whole forms the basic theme of all of Sinclair Lewis's finest novels." Similarly, Frederick Hoffman suggested that there are two Babbitts, one the perfect Menckenese "boob," the other the "doubting Babbitt." A double question follows: can the doubting Babbitt conceive of the qualities that make a man as well as a businessman, that create a society as well as a mere association of "joiners"; and, can Sinclair Lewis? *can anyone?*

The novel makes it easy enough for one to name the values that would save Zenith and Babbitt with it. They are love and friendship; kindness, tolerance, justice, and integrity; beauty; intellect. For the first two of these Babbitt has a throbbing desire if no very large capacity. Of the next four he has intimations. The seventh he can approach only in the distortions of his reveries, as in his morning dream of the "fairy child." To the last he is a total stranger. Of Lewis one may say he was much like Babbitt in the first two, with no greater capacity; that the next four constitute the core of his character and of his demand on life; of the next, that it is too readily softened by sentiment, as is Babbitt's; and of the last one can only say that on the evidence of the novels the matter remains enigmatic) *puzzling*

We have omitted from this list the power of observation, which, in its full sense, may depend on all the other qualities taken together and become the highest form of intuition; but in the more limited sense in which we commonly use the term in both social intercourse and literary discourse, it is this quality that differentiates Lewis from his creature. It is this quality that enabled John O'Hara, many years later, to say that "Lewis was born to write Babbitt's story. . . . All the other novelists and journalists and Babbitt himself were equally blind to Babbitt and Zenith and the United States of America until 1922."

The novel was, in fact, the first of its kind in two striking ways. American literature had a full if brief tradition of the business novel. James, Howells, London, Phillips, Herrick, Sinclair, Wharton, Dreiser, Poole, Tarkington — all these writers had been centrally concerned with the businessman; and, after James and Howells, only Tarkington was to find in him any of the old, perdurable American virtues. Business was synonymous with ethical corruption; the world of business was savagely competitive, brutally aggressive, murderous. The motivation of the businessman was power, money, social prestige — in that order. But the businessman in almost all this fiction was the tycoon, the powerful manufacturer, the vast speculator, the fabulous financier, the monarch of enormous enterprises, the arch-individual responsible only to himself. And his concern was production.

After World War I, the tycoon may still have been the most colorful and dramatic figure in the business myth, but he was no longer the characteristic figure, and *Babbitt* discovers the difference. This is the world of the little businessman and, more particularly, of the middle man. If his morals are no better, his defections are anything but spectacular. Not in the least resembling the autocratic individualist, he is the compromising conformist. No producer himself, his success depends on public relations. He does not rule; he "joins" to be safe. He boosts and boasts with his fellows, sings and cheers in praise of the throng, derides all difference, denounces all dissent — and only to climb with the crowd. And with the supremacy of *public* relations, he abolishes human relations. All this Sinclair Lewis' novel was the first to give back to a culture that was just becoming aware that it could not tolerate what it had made of itself.

And it did it with a difference. The older novels, generally speaking, were solemn or grandly melodramatic denunciations of monstrous figures of aggressive evil. *Babbitt* was raucously satirical of a crowd of ninnies and buffoons who, if they were malicious and mean, were also ridiculous. And yet, along with all that, Babbitt himself was pathetic.

With *Babbitt*, Sinclair Lewis' extraordinary gift for satirical mimicry of American speech found a fuller and more persistent expression than in any previous work. Nowhere is it more successful than in Babbitt's address at the annual meeting of the Zenith Real Estate Board: " 'Some time I hope folks will quit handing all the credit to a lot of moth-eaten, mildewed, out-of-date, old, European dumps, and give proper credit to the famous Zenith spirit, that clean fighting determination to win Success that has made the little old Zip City celebrated in every land and clime, wherever condensed milk and paste-board cartons are known! Believe me, the world has fallen too long for these worn-out countries that aren't producing anything but bootblacks and scenery and booze, that haven't got one bathroom per hundred people, and that don't know a loose-leaf ledger from a slip-cover; and it's just about time for some Zenithite to get his back up and holler for a show-down!' " And so the stream of clotted argot and cliché floods on and on.

With this book, Sinclair Lewis seemed to most readers to have become America's leading novelist. The reviews were extravagant, and the one that seemed to mean most to Lewis himself appeared in the *New Statesman* and was written by Rebecca West. "It has that something extra, over and above," she wrote, "which makes the work of art, and it is signed in every line with the unique personality of the writer." After quoting from one of Babbitt's public speeches, she continues: "It is a bonehead Walt Whitman speaking. Stuffed like a Christmas goose as Babbitt is, with silly films, silly newspapers, silly talk, silly oratory, there has yet struck him the majestic creativeness of his own country, its miraculous power to bear and nourish without end countless multitudes of men and women. . . . But there is in these people a vitality so intense that it must eventually bolt with them and land them willy-nilly into the sphere of intelligence; and this immense commercial machine will become the instrument of their aspiration."

There were dissenting voices among the reviewers. There were those who argued that the vitality of the novel was only the aimless if "unique" vitality of the author himself, and what a critic like Gilbert Seldes, even when praising the book, was really saying was that the imaginative vitality of Sinclair Lewis failed to find any satisfactory aesthetic organization. The whole book should have been rewritten, he argued, after Lewis had taken a long look into himself. The implication was — and it was made explicit by others — that the book had no values beyond Babbitt's own, and that satire, comic and critical as it may be, must found itself on positive standards that are clearly there even if they are not stated. Some critics personalized this view by saying that Lewis himself was Babbitt, and ascribed the success of the novel to the fact that the audience that Lewis satirized recognized in the author not an enemy but an ally, not a teacher but a brother. And, indeed, many of the most loosely enthusiastic reviews that the book received came from the newspapers of those middle-sized middle-western cities that most resembled Zenith and that took pride in having served, as they thought, as the model for that modest metropolis.

If his environment is too powerful for George Babbitt, Lewis' next hero was to prove more powerful than his, and, after the preceding two novels, critics thought again that a "new" Lewis had emerged. In fact, *Arrowsmith* (1925) merely permitted the idealism that had always been present to prevail. The idealist is no longer a solitary figure, for, besides Martin Arrowsmith, there are also Gottlieb, Sondelius, Terry Wickett, and others. These are the dedicated truth seekers, the pure scientists who will not compromise with commercial standards or yield to institutional pres-

17

sures. If, in the end, in order to maintain their own standards, they are forced to withdraw entirely from institutions, their standards are nevertheless victorious.

After *Babbitt*, Lewis had not intended to write a novel about the medical profession. Returning to the Middle West, he was pursuing his intermittent researches for a "labor novel" which he had had in mind ever since his youth. In Chicago he quite accidentally met a young medical research scientist recently associated with the Rockefeller Institute in New York, Paul de Kruif, and together the two discussed the possibility of a novel about the corruptions of the medical profession and of medical research. The idea seized upon Lewis' imagination. His father and brother were both doctors and two of his uncles had been doctors, and while he had already treated the type of the country doctor, he had not dealt with medical science in its grander aspects, and this subject too had long interested him. With De Kruif, he arranged a tour of the Caribbean, where much of the action of *Arrowsmith* was to take place, and then they proceeded to England where Lewis, with De Kruif always at his elbow, began to write the novel. The writing of this novel probably gave him more personal satisfaction than any other that he had already published or that he was to publish. It released a latent strain of idealism that was very powerful in his character but that his other subject matter had not permitted full expression.

The other side of this idealism continued the same as before, and involved the same subjects for satire. A narrow provincialism, hypocrisy, complacency, the "security" of organizational activity, pomposity, the commercial spirit, and the ideal of cash — all these were present again. Their presentation differed not only in that their opposites were given more substantial representation but also in that they were woven into a story that was itself more exciting than any other that Lewis had devised and in that this story

18

included a heroine, Martin's wife Leora, with whom everyone could sympathize, as not everyone could with Carol Kennicott.

The praise for *Arrowsmith*, except for the disgruntled remarks of a few doctors, was universal. In Evanston, Illinois, an obscure young English teacher named Bernard De Voto was able to say what the book was not: it was not urbane, sophisticated, ironical, symmetrical, concise. If it was in some ways naive, so were Hawthorne, Whitman, Mark Twain. And this is what *Arrowsmith* is — America! — in its naiveté no less than its splendor. And thus, trying to tell us what Sinclair Lewis' true quality is, the young critic, as critic, gives up; but not the enthusiastic reader: "It is the most American novel of the generation; and if it is not the best, at least it can never hereafter be out of mind when the few, diverse novels entitled to compete for such an epithet are considered. . . . It goes down to the roots of our day. It is the almost inconceivable pageant of our America. . . . And that will . . . put *Arrowsmith* safely among the permanent accomplishments of its generation — to endure with a few other great novels of America, none of them quite innocent of defect." The voice grows hoarse; it was, the young De Voto confessed within the review, "the most extravagant praise" he had ever written. And he was by no means alone but only a part of the booming chorus. It came as no surprise that this novel, unlike the controversial works that had preceded it, should command the interest of the donors of the Pulitzer prize.

Sinclair Lewis had by this time become a public figure of such quixotic reputation that it came as no great surprise either when he declined to accept the honor. His grounds, not very well argued, were that such prizes tended to legislate taste. Whether or not he was being disingenuous, attempting to punish the Pulitzer people for not having given him the prize for *Main Street* or *Babbitt*, the fact remains that the attendant publicity was worth infinitely more to him than the prize itself or the publicity that he would have received had he accepted it. With this gesture and his next two books, he swiftly reversed the augmented reputation he had won as an idealistic novelist.

The first of these two novels was a piece of hack work, a ridiculous account of adventures in northwest Canada called *Mantrap* (1926), and the second, *Elmer Gantry* (1927), was another explosion, the most controversial of all his books, the most brutal attack on American standards.

Elmer Gantry deals with the shabby area of evangelical religion. Lewis chose Kansas City as the field for his research, and there he cultivated ministers of every denomination and faith. The result was the broadest and the most slashing satire that he was ever to write and the satire least concerned with the presentation of positive values.

Like most of Lewis' novels, *Elmer Gantry* is a loosely episodic chronicle which involves no primary conflict about which all the action is organized, in which value can achieve a complex definition, and by which at least two orders of value are dramatized. The chronicle, like *Babbitt*, breaks down into three large parts, each pretty nearly independent of the others. In each event Elmer's progress is colored and in two of them threatened by his relation with a woman, but from each Elmer emerges triumphant. The first part takes us through his Baptist education, his ordination, his first pulpit, and his escape from Lulu; the second takes us through his career as an evangelist with the fantastic Sharon Falconer; the third takes us through his experience of New Thought and his rise in Methodism, together with the decline of his marriage to Cleo and his escape from Hettie, who threatens to bring him to public ruin but who is herself routed as, in the final sentence, Elmer promises that "We shall yet make these United States a moral nation!"

It should not be supposed that the frank prominence in *Elmer*

Gantry of sexual appetite — a rare enough element in a Lewis novel — or the fact that it several times threatens Elmer's otherwise unimpeded success, in any way provides the kind of dramatized counterpoint on the absence of which we are remarking, or that it in any way serves to introduce an element of human tenderness that modifies Elmer's brutality. On the contrary, it is an integral part of his inhumanity and an integral part of the inhumanity of the religious environment within which he exists. Indeed, of all the forms of relationship that the novel presents, the sexual relation is most undilutedly brutish, and it is perhaps the chief element in that animus of revulsion that motivates the author's creation of this cloacal world.

Hovering on the fringes of the plot are a few figures of good like Frank Shallard, honest clergymen of sincere religious conviction, but these figures, all minor, are never allowed to enter the action or to oppose effectively the major characters, notably Elmer Gantry himself, one of the great beasts of all literature. The minutely detailed history of Elmer Gantry involves an extraordinarily full account of every form of religious decay in American life, an account in which nothing is missing except all religion.

The world of *Elmer Gantry* is a world of total death, of social monsters without shadow. And in some ways therefore the novel gives us the purest Sinclair Lewis. More than this, one may say that, although it caused the greatest furor of all Lewis' novels at the time of publication and although it provided a script for a widely shown film quite recently, it remains the most neglected and perhaps most underestimated of Lewis' major works. For the subject animated in Lewis a latent strain of extravagant fantasy on the one hand, and, on the other, a devastating sense of the possible poverty of human experience. The two moods, nearly opposite and yet clearly counterparts, can be readily illustrated.

The first is best observed in the phantasmagoric scene in which

Sharon capitulates to Elmer before an altar where she associates herself, in a ritual invocation, with all goddesses of fertility:

" 'It is the hour! Blessed Virgin, Mother Hera, Mother Frigga, Mother Ishtar, Mother Isis, dread Mother Astarte of the weaving arms, it is thy priestess, it is she who after the blind centuries and the groping years shall make it known to the world that ye are one, and that in me are ye all revealed, and that in this revelation shall come peace and wisdom universal, the secret of the spheres and the pit of understanding. Ye who have leaned over me and on my lips pressed your immortal fingers, take this my brother to your bosoms, open his eyes, release his pinioned spirit, make him as the gods, that with me he may carry the revelation for which a thousand thousand grievous years the world has panted. . . . O mystical rose, O lily most admirable, O wondrous union; O St. Anna, Mother Immaculate, Demeter, Mother Beneficent, Lakshmi, Mother Most Shining; behold, I am his and he is yours and ye are mine!' "

The absurd extravagance of this scene is somehow emphasized by the absence in it of any honest recognition of human need or of human fulfillment. The travesty that it makes of both the sexual and the religious experience is of course to be associated with the temper of evangelistic orgy that permeates the novel. Dramatically, however, it should be juxtaposed with such an earlier scene, as blankly homely as this one is hilariously horrible — a scene in which a deaf old retired preacher and his wife are going to bed after fifty years of marriage, and the whole of that marital experience is finally equated with the memory of an "old hoss":

" 'I would of liked to had you try your hand at politics. If I could of been, just once, to a senator's house, to a banquet or something, just once, in a nice bright red dress with gold slippers, I'd of been willing to go back to alpaca and scrubbing floors and listening to you rehearsing your sermons, out in the stable, to that old mare we had for so many years — oh, laws, how long is it she's been dead now? Must be — yes, it's twenty-seven years —

" 'Why is it that it's only in religion that the things you got to believe are agin all experience? Now drat it, don't you go and quote that "I believe because it *is* impossible" thing at me again! . . .

" 'Twenty-seven years! And we had that old hoss so long before that. My how she could kick — Busted that buggy —'

"They were both asleep."

The two scenes supplement one another; they represent the extremes of the nightmare image of a world that, totally empty of human value, monstrously, and without relief, parodies the reality.

The book, to the great advantage of its sales, was immediately banned in Boston, and bans of one kind or another — from the simple refusal of public librarians to put it on their shelves, to announcements by booksellers that they would not stock it, to wholesale municipal bans — extended from Kansas City to Camden, from Boston to Glasgow. Every ban provided the publishers with the least expensive form of promotion.

News stories of every kind developed out of the publication of the book and the character of the author. The Boston *Transcript* announced that "it is neither wrong nor unjust to accuse Lewis of being one of the greatest egoists in the world today." He was invited to a lynching party in Virginia; one cleric suggested that a prison sentence of five years was clearly in order. Letters of abuse cluttered his mail.

In a resolution supporting the Anti-Saloon League of New York State, one Methodist minister declared before the annual assemblage of the New York East Conference, "The Methodist Church is cordially hated, not only by the class represented by Mr. Sinclair Lewis and the rum organizations, but also by every evil organization of every kind whatsoever," while only a few weeks later the graduating class of New York University voted Sinclair Lewis its favorite author. An item in an Ohio newspaper ran as follows: "Trouble in the home of Leo Roberts, general manager of the Roberts Coal and Supply Company, began when his wife brought home a copy of *Elmer Gantry* and he burned it as undesirable reading matter, according to Mrs. Roberts at a hearing Wednesday before Judge Bostwick of Probate Court, when Roberts was ordered to a private sanitarium for a short rest, after his wife, Mrs. Margaret Roberts, 1671 Franklin Park South, charged him with lunacy." Very soon ministers' wives were seeking divorces on the grounds that their husbands were Elmer Gantrys, i.e., adulterers; and ministers themselves were demanding that colleagues too attentive to their choir singers be investigated. In less than six weeks, even the least literate of churchgoers had heard the novel denounced from the pulpit of his church.

Never has a profession cooperated so zealously with a publisher as the clergy, of all denominations and faiths, in 1927. Generally, of course, the novel was the subject of denunciation: "slime, pure slime," "sordid and cowardly," "venomous," "unprincipled," "an insult," "filthy" — these were some of the terms of abuse. The evangelist Billy Sunday called Lewis "Satan's cohort." He was not only "Mencken's minion," he was Judas. Yet here and there, quieter clerical voices suggested that, while Elmer Gantry was a monster, the novel itself was a useful tonic in a situation not entirely healthy.

Reviewers praised the novel and abused it with equal vigor. Again, thousands of people bought it. H. L. Mencken thought it one of the great satires of all time and compared Lewis with Voltaire. The novel could not have been more appropriately dedicated than it was — to Mencken, "with profound admiration."

There were to be further reversals. Lewis' first marriage had by now fallen into decay and he was wandering about Europe, alone, looking for new subject matter while the furor over *Elmer Gantry* raged at home. He found his subject matter in the story of a wealthier, more powerful, somewhat more sensitive Babbitt named Samuel Dodsworth, unhappily married, wandering about Europe and discovering a superior woman who would become his second wife. So, stumbling into Berlin, Sinclair Lewis met a superior woman, the handsome Dorothy Thompson, best known newspaperwoman in Europe, and presently she would become his second wife.

He interrupted the writing of *Dodsworth* to expand into a book-length work a short story he had recently published in the *American Mercury* — "The Man Who Knew Coolidge" — the monologue of an idiotic, sub-Babbitt type named Lowell Schmaltz. Exercising here once more his remarkable gift for imitating the speaking American voice, he nevertheless added very little to his stature with this work. Then, after his marriage in London on May 14, 1928, he returned to the United States with his new wife and there finished *Dodsworth* (1929). This work once more assured Lewis' readers that he was a generous man, for while it again had its share of satire, the satire was directed largely at the frenetic pretentiousness and snobbery of Dodsworth's first wife, and it presented Dodsworth himself, with all his solidly American middle-class virtues, in full sympathy. Here there was no occasion at all for controversy. And what Sinclair Lewis himself believed in, at the bottom of his blistered heart, was at last clear: a downright self-reliance, a straightforward honesty, a decent modesty, corn on the cob and apple pie.

The terms of the novel are much the same as they had always been, and the pattern is the same, of the man who glimpses a dream beyond the trivial actualities and stifling habits of his life, and who, now, can make it real. Only the emphasis had been shifted, and the object of satire drastically reversed. Whereas in earlier novels he had satirized the stuffy middle-western citizenry, with its smugness, materialism, and aggressive provinciality, and approved of the "outsiders," Carol and Paul Riesling and Martin Arrowsmith and Frank Shallard, now he satirizes the poor critic of Babbittry that he chooses to give the reader in the character of Fran Dodsworth, and approves the middle-western citizenry in the person of Sam, who has more money than Babbitt and needs, therefore, to think less about it, but who is hardly less aggressive in his own kind of provincialism.

For nearly the first time in his major novels he was handling material that was by no means new — for generations there had been novels about Americans in Europe; but what he was doing, or so it seemed, was new to him: approving the substantial middle-class, middle-western virtues, the best of Babbitt. He had, of course, been doing this all the time and very explicitly in the early, little-read books; but after *Elmer Gantry* and *The Man Who Knew Coolidge*, it seemed a sharp reversal.

No critics observed the larger significance of *Dodsworth* in the career of Sinclair Lewis and in modern American writing. Between the end of the war in 1918 and the beginning of the depression of the 1930's, a revolution had overtaken American life in manners and morals and all intellectual assumptions, and *Main Street, Babbitt, Arrowsmith,* and *Elmer Gantry*, whatever their aesthetic limitations, had played a major part, probably the major literary part, in this transformation. At the end of the 1920's, writers were left either in the situation of Scott Fitzgerald, trying "to hold in balance the sense of futility of effort and the sense of the necessity to struggle," or in the situation of young radicals who tried to turn their writing into social action on behalf of a hypothetical "proletariat." Only extremes of attitude presented themselves as possible: the jaded "aristocratic" attitude implied in the work of

26

Fitzgerald (and implicit in such a school of criticism as the New Humanism, however far this school may have been from him) and the enthusiastic espousal of the revolutionary "working class" attitude exemplified by the *New Masses* and any number of "proletarian" writers. In *Dodsworth*, Lewis refused the extremes and turned back to a reassertion of those very middle-class, middle-brow, and middle-western values that the decade of the twenties seemed to have destroyed forever, and that it had most emphatically modified at least; and with those values he, who would henceforth seem to be the most old-fashioned of modern American novelists, would henceforth abide.

Yet it was the Lewis of *Babbitt* rather than the Lewis of *Dodsworth* that led the Swedish Academy, at the end of 1930, to award him, the first American writer, the Nobel prize in literature. That event followed on the birth of Lewis' second son, Michael, to his second wife, in the middle of that year, and it was probably a considerably less expected event for him. But for some time European readers had been looking with increasing favor on American novelists, and especially on those who, like Sinclair Lewis, were critical of American culture. Other American novelists who were popular in Sweden — Jack London, Upton Sinclair, Edith Wharton, Theodore Dreiser, Sherwood Anderson — were read in much the same spirit as he was, as social critics of the same materialism and chauvinistic complacency, and with no important aesthetic discriminations to be made between them.

Under these circumstances, it is not surprising that Lewis, who was the sharpest and the most detailed critic and who yet wrote out of what seemed to be love of his country, should have come to seem the leader. He had come to seem the leader, however, of a body of literature that was in itself as exciting as any in the world, and a body of literature that, in its very criticism of American culture, demonstrated its maturity.

That criticism Lewis brought to its climax in his famous address delivered in Stockholm on December 12, 1930, and known now under the title "The American Fear of Literature." An attack on the atrophied tradition of gentility and academicism in American critical values, it announced that "Our American professors like their literature clear and cold and pure and very dead." Rather unfairly, it placed the blame on the continuing prestige of William Dean Howells (who had, in fact, been gracious to the still unknown young Lewis in their single encounter in 1916), and, defying "official" custodians of American literary culture, such as the American Academy of Arts and Letters, it praised such dissident novelists as Theodore Dreiser and Sherwood Anderson, and brought to the attention of its European audience the names of a whole group of young American writers who were still almost entirely unknown abroad. There are fallacies as well as injustices in the address, but it was composed in an authoritative spirit that made Lewis, on that day, in that year, the spokesman — what Walt Whitman had called the "literatus" — for the literary culture of the United States.

If Sinclair Lewis' reception of the Nobel prize was the historic event — and his spokesman-like acceptance of it only the marker of the event — its historic import was not merely in its putting American literature on a par with any other literature in the world, but also in its acknowledging that in the world America was a power that twenty years before it had not been, and that, until now, Europe had been reluctant to concede that it was. In December 1930 Sinclair Lewis was bigger than America knew; proud as he may have been — and he was proud, above all, because he was regarded as of equal importance with three eminent scientists — he was bigger than even he himself knew, or would ever know. Or should we say that he was a smaller writer than he thought and a much larger symbol?

In Berlin early in 1931, in a fit of pique that climaxed long brooding, Lewis wrote his publisher, Alfred Harcourt, of Harcourt, Brace, and Company in New York, to tell him that their connection was severed. For a long time, he wrote Harcourt, he had felt that the firm had lost real interest in his books, and its failure to rise to the occasion of the Nobel prize had made its indifference all too clear. With proper advertising of the event, all his novels would have leaped into soaring sales figures again, Lewis announced. Worse than that, Harcourt had done nothing, even though he had the whole European press at his disposal, to counteract the supercilious and denigrating remarks about Lewis in the American press. "If you haven't used this opportunity to push my books energetically and to support my prestige intelligently, you never will do so, because I can never give you again such a moment."

Alfred Harcourt released him from his contractual obligations without any attempt to meet his charges. He may very well have felt that the separation came at a logical time. The decade through which Harcourt, Brace, and Company had helped to make Sinclair Lewis an international reputation, and in the course of which Lewis' novels had helped to make of Harcourt, Brace, and Company a substantial firm, was over. Throughout that decade Lewis had promulgated his version of the American reality, and his effort had been brought to a climax with the great honor. But the decade was over, and Lewis' sense of reality was no longer central to American history. He would never be able to change that sense, but history had already changed and would continue to change in his time, leaving him uneasily behind. His own discomforted sense of the change and of his inability to cope with current history as confidently as he had coped with the past may very well have been the major ingredient in his dissatisfaction with his publisher. His novels would continue to make money, and there would be many more of them, but they would never again bring distinction to a publisher's list as, in a succession of five smashing titles, they had brought to Harcourt, Brace, and Company. The Nobel prize had come to him at precisely the right moment: it was the moment at which Lewis, the serious novelist, was finished.

He was now forty-six years old and the author of twelve published novels. There were to be twenty more years and ten more novels. The beguilements of alcohol, which had for some time been a problem for him, would become an increasingly acute problem as these twenty years passed. His second marriage would fall into even more sordid decay than had his first. His first son would be killed in World War II. His second son would grow up to be a not very successful actor and would justify his own peccadilloes in adolescence and irresponsibilities in maturity by the example of the conduct of his father. Lewis, an increasingly restless man, would move from one establishment to another, from one city to another, all over the world, briefly occupying magnificent houses which, after a few months or a year or two at most, he would sell at great financial loss, when he would move on again in the hope of finding a better place. Precisely like his characters, he was always pursuing some vague and undefined glimmer of a happier place, a richer life.

How far he had moved, in these splendid establishments, from his humble beginnings in Sauk Centre! And yet there was always something bleak and unlived-in about even his most lavish houses that suggested all too clearly that the bleakness of Sauk Centre still clung to him and lived on deep within him. How far, too, his international literary reputation had removed him from those taunts and jibes that had plagued him in his youth and young manhood, and yet he felt himself still the victim of taunts and jibes, never really taken seriously as an artist, he felt, by other artists. In a kind of mounting frenzy he sought out the comforts of women much younger than he, especially young actresses, during a period when he was infatuated with writing for the stage and even took to acting himself, and finally, at the end of the 1930's and for a time in the 1940's, he did find a young actress who was willing to try to comfort him. But in some profound way he was not to be comforted or consoled, and after the young woman abandoned him to marry a man more nearly her own age, Lewis began a series of restless wanderings in Europe, and there, finally, in 1951, he was to die alone, among strangers, in Roman ostentation. But all through those maddening years of decline, he continued, with a kind of mechanical regularity and even ruthlessness, to produce his novels.

The first of these was *Ann Vickers*, published in 1933 — the story of an American career woman, and already, so soon after his second marriage, shot through with all his ambiguities of feeling about the career of his new wife, which was to be phenomenally successful through all that decade and into the next. The novel attempts, through a large part of the life of a single character, to sketch in the chief interests in a whole period of American social history from before World War I into the Great Depression. For this history, Lewis drew largely on the background of his new wife's life but partly as well on that of his own earlier years — prewar Christian socialism, feminism and settlement house work, charity organizations, liberal and radical thought, prison reform, sexual emancipation, the crisis of the depression, careers for women, equal rights, and so on. Through it all is the recurrent theme of a woman who is trying to find herself as a woman, not only as a Great Woman, just as *Dodsworth* was the story of a man trying to find himself as a man within the Businessman.

What is probably most interesting about the novel is the author's own ambiguous feeling about his heroine — exactly the feeling that he was already developing about Dorothy Thompson. Having chosen her as the prototype of Ann Vickers, he put himself in the position of describing sympathetically qualities that he was already resenting in life. His approval of Ann's dedication to "do-good" principles is at least uneasy; he resents the liberal and radical causes that his own characterization of her committed him to approve; the satiric touches are sporadic and sprawling, settling on her, on him, on them, but never pulling these together into real satire at all. Most interesting is the portrait of Ann's husband, a feeble fellow who is jealous of her expansiveness and prestige. Ann is rescued from this marriage by a man with red hair — Sinclair Lewis was famous for his red hair and was nicknamed "Red" — but he bears no other resemblance to Sinclair Lewis, is, rather, quite his opposite — a kind of dream figure of warm tolerance and relaxed sensuality that Lewis would have liked to be but had never been and would never be able to be.

Work of Art (1934), the next novel, was probably the first of Lewis' serious novels since *Main Street* to be completely without distinction. (By "serious" one means work that he himself took seriously.) This novel brings to a climax, certainly, his old, uneasy suspicion of intellect and art, and his deep respect for middle-class virtue, for effort. A novel about the hotel industry in America, it deals with two brothers, Myron and Ora Weagle. Myron is steady and reliable and, even as a boy, dreams of some day owning a perfect hotel. Ora is "literary" and spends his good-for-nothing days mooning in romantic fantasies and in writing verse of much the same sort as Sinclair Lewis wrote as a boy and a young man, and this portrait, a fantastic caricature of the Poet, is Lewis' belated act of exorcism. Ora grows up to be a commercial success and a hack, always self-deluded and scornful of his downright brother. But Myron is the true artist, and Lewis makes nearly his every effort analogous to an act of artistic creation. Ultimately, Myron even keeps a notebook, "what must, in exactness, be called 'The Notebook of a Poet,'" in which he jots down ideas for improving hotel management and reflections upon his experience as a hotelkeeper. Myron, too, has great success, then through the chicanery of others falls to low estate, and recovers when he concludes that no hotel can be perfect but that he can still make a "work of art" of a tourist camp in Kansas. If one wishes to learn about hotel management the novel is no doubt an admirable handbook, and no duller than a handbook; if one wishes to learn anything about art, and especially the art of the novel, there is nothing here at all. *Work of Art* is the fantasy of the perfect Rotarian. It is almost as if George F. Babbitt had suddenly produced a novel.

It was no longer the best of the middle-class character that Sinclair Lewis was praising, but the very middle of the middle. His wife, in a few years, had gained a tremendous reputation on the international scene as a political commentator, and the greater her authority grew and the brighter the glamour that clung to it, the deeper Lewis drove himself back into the defensive but pathetic aggressiveness of Sauk Centre. If he ever divorced his wife, he is reputed to have said, he would name Adolf Hitler as corespondent. But he could not have written his next novel, *It Can't Happen Here* (1935), if he had not been intimately exposed to her intense interest in international affairs, a subject the discussion of which, he continually complained, would drive him out of his wits.

At least one of Lewis' novels after *It Can't Happen Here* was to make more money for him, but no other was to cause such excitement. In this book, it seemed, he was at his greatest: denouncing the Fascist elements in American life, praising the independent spirit, holding out for freedom. In 1935 the United States was being heckled on every side by absurd demagogues like Huey Long, and Lewis, seizing on this proliferation of the totalitarian impulse, which did seem to pose a serious threat to the democratic traditions and promises of American life, translated it into the terms of political establishment. The horror of fascism in Europe and local imitations were enough to persuade many readers that Lewis had written an impressively prophetic work.

What he had in fact written was a tour de force in which he simply documented the transformation of traditional American political and social customs into their opposites. Doremus Jessup, the hero, driven into his heroic stance at the end of the novel, is not really very different from Lewis' next hero, Fred Cornplow, of *The Prodigal Parents* (1938). *It Can't Happen Here* elicited considerable excitement among left-wing sympathizers who could, from this novel, be assured that Lewis was not a Fascist; but *The Prodigal Parents* — a miserable novel — gave these sympathizers small comfort, for in this book Lewis defended the stuffiest middle-class attitudes against the silliest "proletarian" views.

Considered as a whole work, *It Can't Happen Here* differs from other examples of the genre in having neither the intellectual coherence of Aldous Huxley in *Brave New World* nor the persuasive vision of a nightmare future of George Orwell in *1984*. But in 1935 readers in the United States, like readers in Britain and in France (*Impossible Ici!*), were sensitive to their immediate history, and it was to the immediate possibility of that history that Lewis' novel shook their attention. Yet to have seen the novel as committing Sinclair Lewis to what was then called the United Front — the collaborative effort of all liberal and radical parties against the threat of fascism — was an error; for Lewis, while once a socialist and still a liberal of sorts, was certainly in no sense a political radical. This fact became abundantly clear in the next novel, that sad effort of *The Prodigal Parents*. This story of Fred Cornplow and his wife Hazel, in revolt from their foolishly radical and irresponsible children, brings to a lame end, no doubt, Lewis' one-time ambition to write a novel about political idealism. Radical politics are parodied in the figure of a comic-strip Communist and through the vagaries of undergraduates whose absurd concern with the problems of labor is apparently the net result of Lewis' observation of liberal student attitudes in the United States during the 1930's, when he lived in the neighborhood of Dartmouth College. Against these feeble antagonists is set the good American, Cornplow, a stodgy bundle of received opinions, the stereotype approved.

Now, at the end of the fourth decade of the twentieth century, with the United States about to plunge into another world war and a rather different kind from the first, Sinclair Lewis was only a confused man. Retreating into the absorbing life of the theater and devoting himself to the pursuit of young actresses, he turned, not surprisingly, to frivolous subjects in a half dozen unsuccessful plays and in his next novel. *Bethel Merriday* (1940) is a novel about a young actress. Less embarrassing than *The Prodigal Parents*, it is hardly more important as fiction. Through the education of his young heroine in summer stock and touring companies, Lewis was able to include everything that he had learned about the theater; attached to rather than incorporated in this handbook material is a pale romance. Learning as much as one does of the theater, one learns nothing of the impulses that drive an actor or of the kind of satisfactions that an actor finds in his profession; and while the novel at one point glances at a May and December relationship, one learns no more of Sinclair Lewis' passion for young women than for the stage.

Gideon Planish (1943), the novel that followed, seemed to promise something of a return to the old Lewis. While he apparently intended, in this satiric attack on organized philanthropy and the activities of liberal "do-gooders," a return to the savage mode of *Elmer Gantry*, he achieved in fact little more than a crude parody and none of the solidity of that earlier novel. A splenetic attack, arising from the narrowest channels of a provincial mind, on the efforts of the professional "intellectual," its satire deteriorates into farce very soon after the novel gets under way. One figure in the book, Winifred Homeward, "the Talking Woman," a cartoon-like take-off of his newly divorced wife, only underlined the essential lack of seriousness that characterizes this novel. And yet, self-deluded, Sinclair Lewis was able to autograph a copy of this work with the inscription "My most serious book — therefore, naturally, not taken too seriously."

That he intended to be serious in *Gideon Planish*, at least at the outset, one cannot doubt; but it is something of a relief to turn to the next novel, *Cass Timberlane* (1945), with its much less serious subject. A novel about American marriage, it is half-sentimental, half-splenetic. It is his own thinly veiled love story, or rather, an extrapolation of such little love story as he had to tell; and from this situation arose his chief novelistic difficulties. Cass Timberlane is presented as forty-one years old, in love with a girl of twenty-three; but he behaves in some ways like a man of sixty, which Lewis now was, and in others like a fumbling boy of sixteen, which he also was. Cass's most remarkable quality — which goes unremarked in the novel itself — is his sexual naiveté, and when the young Jinny Marshland leaves him and enjoys an adulterous affair with his contemporary and best friend, it is not, the reader can only assume, his age that has been his problem.

The story of Cass and Jinny is treated with a kind of sentimental affection, with only the faintest overtones of irony, and its treatment marks it off very sharply from the treatment of marriage in a whole group of surrounding sketches which the novel presents under the heading of "An Assemblage of Husbands and Wives." In these often brutally conceived accounts of female willfulness, tyranny, and lechery, the recognition of the American matriarchy is as clear as the method is uncompromisingly satirical. It is as if the novelist is trying to say two things at once, that all these

are American marriages in general, including his own two marriages, but that this one at the center, of Cass and Jinny, is another
matter, the marriage that he would now make if he could. With
the slightest change of method — that is to say, with the slightest
shift in perspective on his own situation — that central marriage
would become only another in the great assemblage of miserable
marriages at large. But one must remember that even Lewis' best
novels were not notable for their clarity of point of view or for
their power of self-evaluation. Should one expect these of him at
sixty, infatuated?

And so he staggered toward his end. In *Kingsblood Royal* (1947)
he made his last strenuous effort to re-enter American realities
by addressing himself to the problem of the Negro minority in
American life. The book aroused some excitement as a social document but none whatever as a literary performance, and even its
social usefulness, it is now clear, is minimized by Lewis' mechanical
oversimplification of what is, of course, one of the most complex,
as well as one of the most pressing, issues in the national life of
the United States. From this attempt to deal with the immediate
present, Lewis retreated into the historical past of Minnesota.
The God-Seeker (1949) is apparently the first part of what was
finally projected as a trilogy about labor in the United States. But
it is a wooden, costumed performance about which even Lewis'
faithful publishers despaired. And his last novel, *World So Wide*,
published posthumously in 1951 (he died on January 10 of that
year), is a thin attempt to write another *Dodsworth*. It is the final
self-parody. As Malcolm Cowley wrote, his characters sound now
"like survivors from a vanished world, like people just emerging
from orphanages and prisons where they had listened for thirty
years to nothing but tape recordings of Lewis novels."

As he had experienced a long and unrewarding apprenticeship
before his phenomenal, ten-year success, so he suffered a long and

sad decline. This beginning and this end do not make easy the problem of delivering any final literary judgment on Sinclair Lewis. The estimate of his literary contemporaries, which became so apparent at the time of the Nobel award, does not make the problem any easier.

The aggressively enlightened had, of course, almost never taken him seriously. The experimentalists and the expatriates thought of him as a commercial hack. The academic critics, whether simple literary historians like Fred L. Pattee, or dogmatic authoritarians like Professor Irving Babbitt and his followers in the New Humanism, or old-fashioned conservatives like Henry Van Dyke in the American Academy of Arts and Letters — they were united in their displeasure with the award. "Nothing [Lewis] can write can matter much now," Professor Pattee had just pontificated in *The New American Literature*, and the brilliant young liberal critic T. K. Whipple had just published his damaging estimate (one of the few genuinely critical appraisals of Lewis up to that time, and up to this) in his book called *Spokesmen*. Young radicals found Lewis politically illiterate. Older writers of no particular allegiance, like Sherwood Anderson, spoke out against him on the grounds of art. A younger writer, Ernest Hemingway, writing to a friend, called the award a filthy business whose only merit was that it had eliminated the "Dreiser menace." Dreiser held Lewis in gross and sullen contempt.

This is all rather cruel because Lewis himself was among the most generous of men in his relations with other writers. He encouraged the young and struggling with praise and with money. He habitually put the men who had chosen him as their enemy, Dreiser and Anderson, at the very head of his list of the greatest modern American writers. He recognized early the brilliant quality of the young Ernest Hemingway and he was instrumental in getting an award for the mature Hemingway as he was for getting a large cash prize for Theodore Dreiser. He in effect "discovered" Thomas Wolfe for the world when, only a year after the publication of *Look Homeward, Angel*, Lewis spoke of this book at a press conference before departing for Sweden and mentioned Wolfe again in the Nobel speech itself.

And it is quite true, of course, that even his most famous novels have crass defects. He was, in the first place, the kind of writer who found it temperamentally impossible to objectify his own anxieties, the tensions of his inner life, or even to draw upon them except in the most superficial way, in his own writing, and the writer, after all, is not different from the man who contains him. Shunning the subjective, he often fell into the sentimental. Yet there are other realities than those that pertain to the subjective life. His twenty-two novels, so uneven in quality, do share in one likeness: they are a long march all directed toward a single discovery, the "reality" of America. This aim was Lewis' inheritance as a novelist who was formed in the second decade of this century, when the discovery of the "real" America, an America beyond the chauvinistic nonsense and the merely sentimental optimism that had formed the image of an earlier generation, became the aim of nearly every writer who took himself seriously. It was a period that, however briefly, put its trust in the democratic promise of American life. For Sinclair Lewis, America was always promises, and that was why, in 1950, he could say that he loved America but did not like it, for it was still only promises, and promises that nearly everyone else had long ago given up. Sinclair Lewis had nothing else to turn to.

There is a personal as well as a cultural basis for this situation. For what were these promises? They were promises, first of all, of a society that from his beginning would have not only tolerated but treasured *him*. That is the personal basis. Generalized, it becomes an idealization of an older America, the America of the mid-nineteenth century, an America enormous and shapeless but overflowing, like a cornucopia, with the potentialities for and the constant expression of a wide, casually human freedom, the individual life lived in honest and perhaps eccentric effort (all the better for that), the social life lived in a spirit that first of all tolerates variety and individual difference. It was the ideal America of Thoreau, of Whitman, of the early Mark Twain, of the cracker barrel in the village store and of the village atheist, of the open road and the far horizon and the clear, uncluttered sweep of prairies. Like Thoreau, Whitman, Twain, Lewis too could see the difference between the idealization and the actuality. It was Thoreau who wrote this indictment: "With respect to true culture and manhood, we are essentially provincial still, not metropolitan — mere Jonathans. We are provincial, because we do not find at home our standards; because we are warped and narrowed by an exclusive devotion to trade and commerce and manufacture and agriculture and the like, which are but the means, and not the ends."

Sinclair Lewis was always carrying around the works of Thoreau. When he claimed him as the major influence on his work, it could have been only this basic element in his own thought, the Thoreauvian ideal of individual freedom and native integrity, that he had in mind.

Of Thoreau, R. W. B. Lewis has written in *The American Adam* as follows: "Probably nobody of his generation had a richer sense of the potentiality for a fresh, free, and uncluttered existence; certainly no one projected the need for a ritual burning of the past in more varied and captivating metaphors. This is what *Walden* is about; it is the most searching contemporary account of the desire for a new kind of life . . . the total renunciation of the traditional, the conventional, the socially acceptable, the well-worn paths of conduct, and the total immersion in nature."

All of this, item by item, even to the last, not only appealed to Sinclair Lewis but in fact formed the positive element in his largely negative presentation of American life. And into that idealism it was not difficult to weave the more diluted optimism that he had found in the novels of the other literary figure who profoundly influenced him, H. G. Wells — the happy belief that the little man, the obscure man, the middle-class man, the outsider like the young Lewis, could break into such freedom as Thoreau envisaged. This was the motive of Lewis' life as it was of his fiction. Deep under the quixotic social conduct, and deep under the satire of social surfaces lay this ambition and this yearning.

The American defection from the American potentiality for individual freedom is the large subject of Lewis' satire. When he excoriated Americans it was because they would not be free, and he attacked all the sources by means of which they betrayed themselves into slavery: the economic system, intellectual rigidity, theological dogma, legal repression, class convention, materialism, social timidity, hypocrisy, affectation, complacency, and pomposity. These two, the individual impulse to freedom and the social impulse to restrict it, provide the bases of his plots in novel after novel. Even when he used Europe as his point of contrast, the conflict was not so much between American and European values as between the true America as Lewis saw it — that is, individual Americans true to their individuality — and the false America, or Americans who yield to values not their own or to values of less amplitude than their own should be. The result in the novels is often an apparent praise of provincialism, even of a deplorable Philistinism, but in its impulse the praise is of something much larger and of something rather noble.

But he was himself sentimental and a Philistine, and often these led him to settle for the very stolidity in American life that he flayed. "Sinclair Lewis is the most successful critic of American society," T. K. Whipple said, "because he is himself the best proof that his charges are just." If he was the village intellectual, the village atheist, the rebel, the nonconformist crank for whom the dialect, the cracker barrel, and the false whiskers served as counterpoise to the stuffed shirt in his defense of what Lloyd Morris called "the old, free, democractic, individualistic career of the middle class," he was at the same time the pontifical village banker, the successful manufacturer of automobiles, the conservative, the very middle of the middle. His trust in "culture" was equaled by his trust in "things." His respect for science was certainly greater than his respect for art. Brought up in an environment that condescended to art and reverenced success, he managed, in that America, to make a success of "art." Often and increasingly it was bad art, and the success was in many ways abrasive and self-destructive. In his novels, he loved what he lamented; in his life, he was most secure and content with the kind of people who might have been the prototypes for his own creatures.

Ten years before his death, in a mock obituary, he said of himself that he had "affected but little the work of younger writers of fiction," that his style and his conception of the novel had in no way altered the contours of the American literary tradition. One can only wonder whether he had any sense at all of how increasingly old-fashioned he came to sound, or that the generation immediately following upon his own — Fitzgerald, Hemingway, Faulkner — was in fact quite a different generation which his work could in almost no way impinge upon, that he spoke for an older American experience than theirs. But in a larger sense than is suggested by the most familiar words in our critical vocabulary, *style* and *structure*, *symbol* and *strategy*, *tone* and *tension* and *intention*, he was an extraordinary influence, the major figure, probably, in what is called the liberation of modern American literature.

42

He had other impressive qualities, among them the ability to create a gallery of characters who have independent life outside the novels, with all their obvious limitations — characters that live now in the American historical tradition. A number of them have become gigantic, archetypal figures that embody the major traits of their class. Lewis' novels, as a result, are perhaps the last important American novels that are primarily concerned with social class. Or are John Marquand and John O'Hara and James Gould Cozzens of his stature? If Lewis' novels often depended more heavily than theirs on the mere report of social minutiae and of the details of the American lingo and more often failed to realize that material imaginatively, they nevertheless — as Joseph Wood Krutch has said — "recorded a reign of grotesque vulgarity which but for him would have left no record of itself because no one else could have adequately recorded it."

He performed a function that has nearly gone out of American fiction, and American fiction is thinner for the loss. Many American novelists today tell us about our subjective lives, and on that subject Sinclair Lewis could hardly speak at all. Fitzgerald, Hemingway, Faulkner — they all had some sense of the tragic nature of human experience that was denied to Lewis. Lyric joy, sensuous ecstasy — to these, too, he was apparently a stranger. But he had a stridently comic gift of mimicry that many a more polished American writer does not have at all. And a vision of a hot and dusty hell: the American hinterland. He gave Americans their first shuddering glimpses into a frightening reality of which until he wrote they were unaware and of which he himself may also have been unaware. As Alfred Kazin wrote: "There is indeed more significant terror of a kind in Lewis's novels than in a writer like Faulkner or the hard-boiled novelists, for it is the terror immanent in the commonplace, the terror that arises out of the repression, the meannesses, the hard jokes of the world Lewis had soaked into his pores." With that America "soaked into his pores," he could document for an enormous audience the character of a people and a class, and, without repudiating either, criticize and laugh uproariously at both. In any strict literary sense, he was not a great writer, but without his writing one cannot imagine modern American literature. No more, without his writing, could Americans today imagine themselves. His epitaph should be: *He did us good.*

⤴ *Selected Bibliography*

orks of Sinclair Lewis

ır Mr. Wrenn: The Romantic Adventures of a Gentle Man. New York:
Harper, 1914.
ıe Trail of the Hawk: A Comedy of the Seriousness of Life. New York: Harper,
ı915.
ıe Job: An American Novel. New York: Harper, 1917.
ıe Innocents: A Story for Lovers. New York: Harper, 1917.
ee Air. New York: Harcourt, Brace, and Howe, 1919.
ıin Street: The Story of Carol Kennicott. New York: Harcourt, Brace, 1920.
bbitt. New York: Harcourt, Brace, 1922.
rowsmith. New York: Harcourt, Brace, 1925.
ıntrap. New York: Harcourt, Brace, 1926.
ner Gantry. New York: Harcourt, Brace, 1927.
*ıe Man Who Knew Coolidge: Being the Soul of Lowell Schmaltz, Constructive
ınd Nordic Citizen*. New York: Harcourt, Brace, 1928.
dsworth. New York: Harcourt, Brace, 1929.
n Vickers. New York: Doubleday, Doran, 1933.
ırk of Art. New York: Doubleday, Doran, 1934.
ected Short Stories. New York: Doubleday, Doran, 1935.
ıhawker: A Play in Three Acts (written with Lloyd Lewis). New York:
Doubleday, Doran, 1935.
Can't Happen Here. New York: Doubleday, Doran, 1935.
e Prodigal Parents. New York: Doubleday, Doran, 1938.
ıhel Merriday. New York: Doubleday, Doran, 1940.
ıeon Planish. New York: Doubleday, Doran, 1943.
ıs Timberlane: A Novel of Husbands and Wives. New York: Random House,
ı945.
ıgsblood Royal. New York: Random House, 1947.
e God-Seeker. New York: Random House, 1949.
ırld So Wide. New York: Random House, 1951.
ım Main Street to Stockholm: Letters of Sinclair Lewis, 1919–1930, edited by
Harrison Smith. New York: Harcourt, Brace, 1952.
e Man from Main Street: Selected Essays and Other Writings, 1904–1950,
:dited by Harry E. Maule and Melville H. Cane. New York: Random House,
ı953.

Current American Reprints

Ann Vickers. New York: Dell. $.75.
Arrowsmith. New York: Signet Classics (New American Library). $.75.
Babbitt. New York: Signet Classics. $.75.
Cass Timberlane. New York: Bantam. $.75.
Dodsworth. New York: Dell. $.75.
Elmer Gantry. New York: Dell. $.60.
Gideon Planish. New York: Popular Library. $.50.
The God-Seeker. New York: Popular Library. $.60.
I'm a Stranger Here Myself. (Short stories selected by Mark Schorer, with an Introduction.) New York: Dell. $.50.
It Can't Happen Here. New York: Dell. $.60.
Kingsblood Royal. New York: Popular Library. $.50.
Main Street. New York: Signet Classics. $.75.
World So Wide. New York: Pyramid. $.35.

Critical and Biographical Studies

Grebstein, Sheldon Norman. *Sinclair Lewis*. (United States Authors Series.) New York: Twayne, 1962.

Guthrie, Ramon. "Sinclair Lewis and the 'Labor Novel,'" *Proceedings* (Second Series, Number 2), American Academy of Arts and Letters. New York, 1952. (An interesting account of Lewis' attempt to write his labor novel.)

———. "The 'Labor Novel' That Sinclair Lewis Never Wrote," *New York Herald Tribune Books*, February 10, 1952. (A shorter version of the preceding.)

"Harrison, Oliver" (Harrison Smith). *Sinclair Lewis*. New York: Harcourt, Brace, 1925. (A promotion piece commissioned by Lewis' publisher.)

Lewis, Grace Hegger. *Half a Loaf*. New York: Liveright, 1931. (This novel by Lewis' first wife is a bizarre *roman à clef*.)

———. *With Love from Gracie*. New York: Harcourt, Brace, 1955. (A biographical memoir following closely *Half a Loaf*.)

Manson, Alexander (as told to Helen Camp). "The Last Days of Sinclair Lewis," *Saturday Evening Post*, 223:27, 110–12 (March 31, 1951). (An account by Lewis' last secretary, much less effective than Perry Miller's.)

Miller, Perry. "The Incorruptible Sinclair Lewis," *Atlantic*, 187:30–34 (April 1951). (A persuasively written impression of Lewis' last days in Florence.)

Schorer, Mark. *Sinclair Lewis: An American Life*. New York: McGraw-Hill, 1961. (Contains a reliable check list of Lewis' publications.)

———, ed. *Sinclair Lewis: A Collection of Critical Essays*. (Twentieth Century Views.) Englewood Cliffs, N.J.: Prentice-Hall (Spectrum Books), 1962. (The best critical writing about Lewis is contained in this collection.)

Sherman, Stuart Pratt. *The Significance of Sinclair Lewis.* New York: Harcourt, Brace, 1922. (A promotion piece commissioned by Lewis' publishers.)
Thompson, Dorothy. "Boy and Man from Sauk Centre," *Atlantic,* 206:39–48 (November 1960). (A touching piece of reminiscent speculation.)
Van Doren, Carl. *Sinclair Lewis: A Biographical Sketch.* With a Bibliography by Harvey Taylor. New York: Doubleday, Doran, 1933. (A promotion piece commissioned by Lewis' publisher; the bibliography is highly unreliable.)